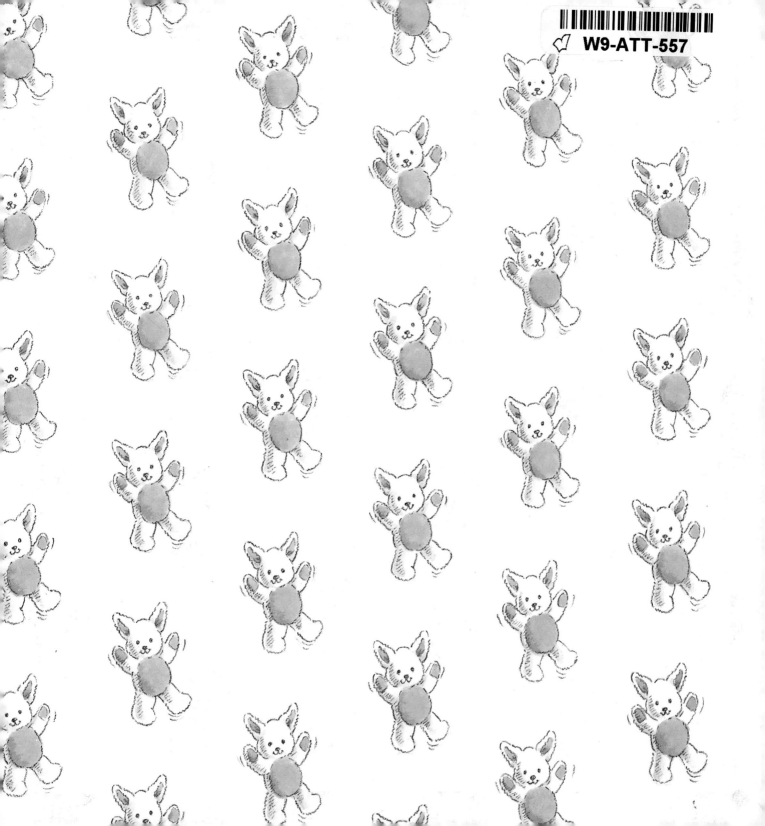

dedicated to Christopher Henry

First edition for the United States, Canada, and the Philippines published 1988 by Barron's Educational Series, Inc.

Text © Copyright Frances Lincoln, Ltd., 1988.
Illustrations © Copyright Edwina Riddell, 1988.

100 First Words was conceived, edited and designed by Frances Lincoln Limited,
Apollo Works, 5 Charlton Kings Road,
London NW5, England

Design and art direction Debbie MacKinnon
Editors Pippa Rubinstein, Sarah Mitchell

All enquiries should be addressed to:
Barron's Educational Series, Inc.
250 Wireless Boulevard
Hauppauge, New York 11788

Library of Congress Catalog Card No. 87-35217

International Standard Book No. 0-8120-5786-4

Library of Congress Cataloging-in-Publication Data
Riddell, Edwina.
    100 first words to say with your baby / illustrated by Edwina Riddell. — 1st ed. for the U.S., Canada, and the Philippines.
        p. cm.
    Summary: Introduces basic vocabularly through labeled pictures of familiar objects.
    ISBN 0-8120-5786-4
    I. Vocabulary – Juvenile literature.   [1. Vocabulary.]   I. Title.
II. Title: One hundred first words to say with your baby.
III. Title: Hundred first words to say with your baby.
PE1449.R53 1988
428.1 – dc 19   87-35217
                                                                          CIP
                                                                          AC

Printed in Hong Kong

890   987654321

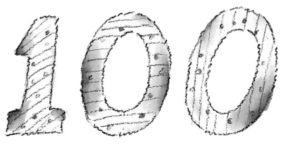

100
first words
to say with your baby

Edwina Riddell

BARRON'S

Grandma

Mommy

baby

Daddy

boy

Grandpa

girl

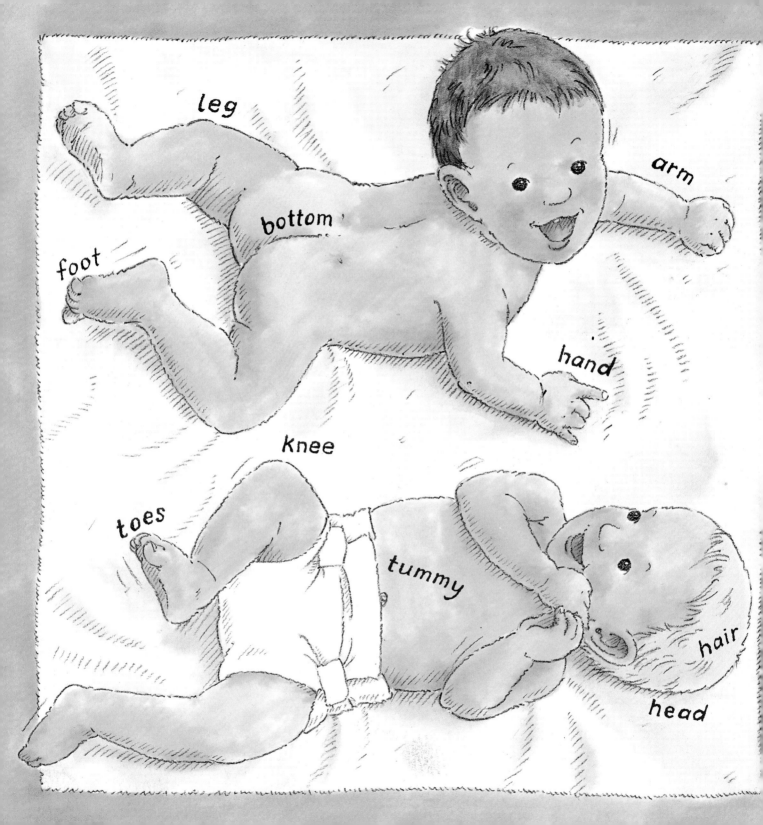

leg

arm

bottom

foot

hand

knee

toes

tummy

hair

head

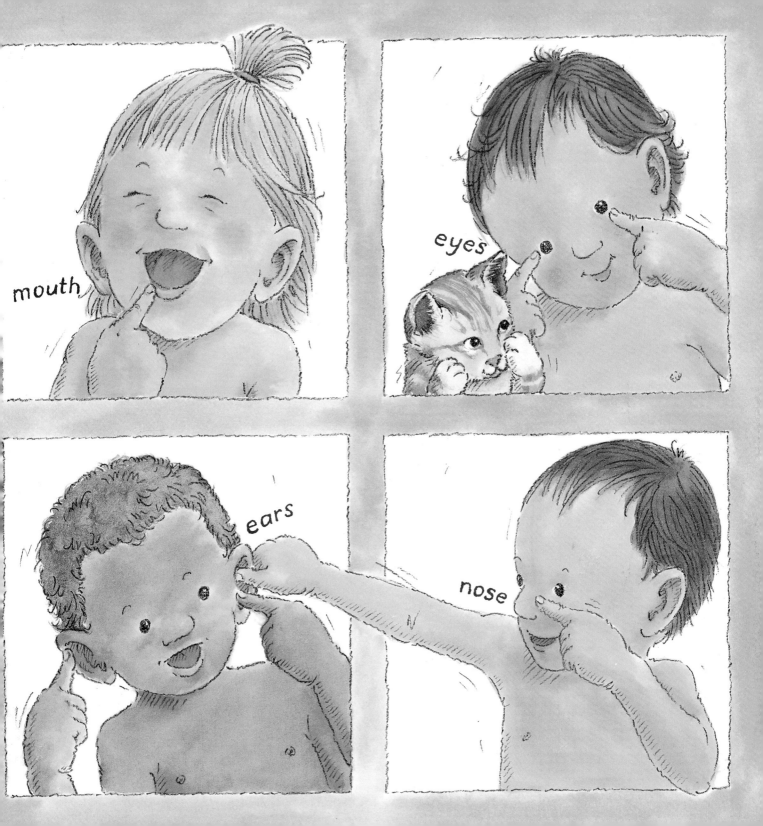

jacket

overalls

gloves

boots

shoes

sweater

panties

hat

undershirt

socks

diaper

dress

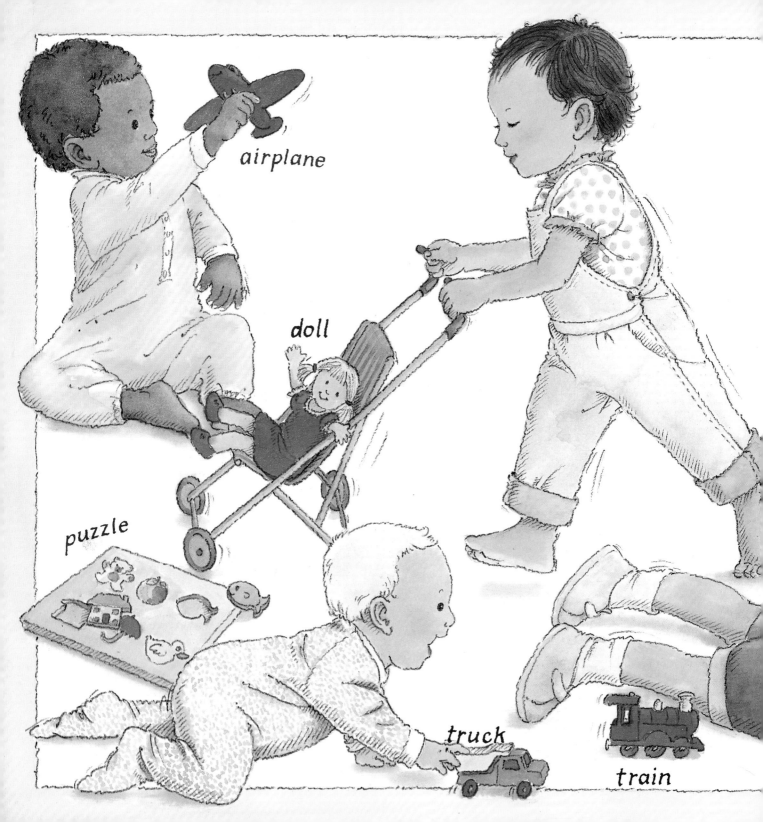

airplane

doll

puzzle

truck

train

blocks

tricycle

crayon

paper

telephone

water

boat

ball

swimsuit

fish

tube

sun hat

Sand

pail

shovel

shells

car

car seat

window

door

wheel

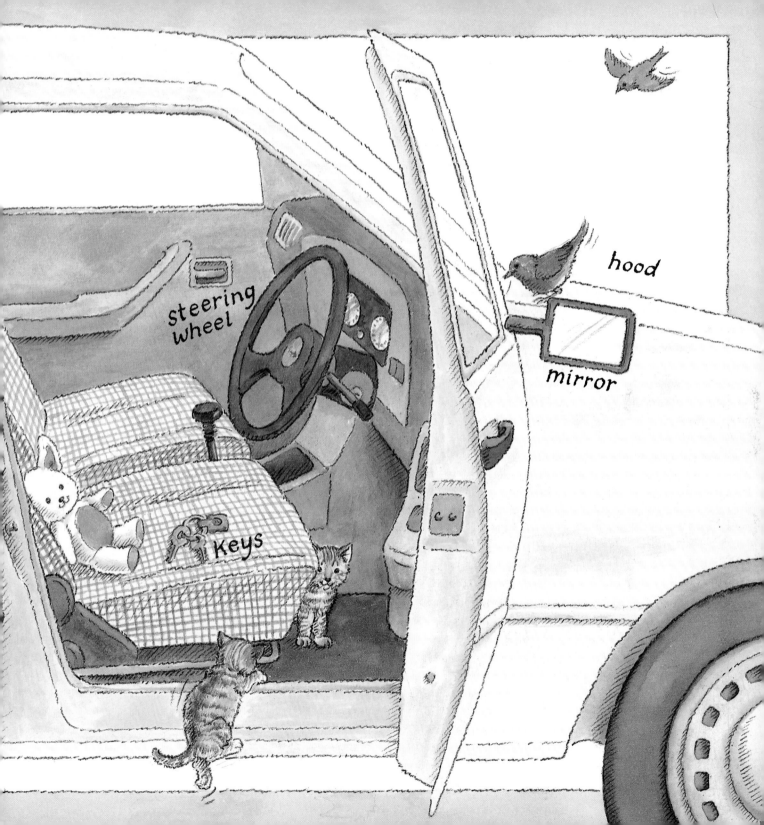

steering
wheel

hood

mirror

Keys

shelves

bread

cart

bottle

cash register

cans

eggs

box

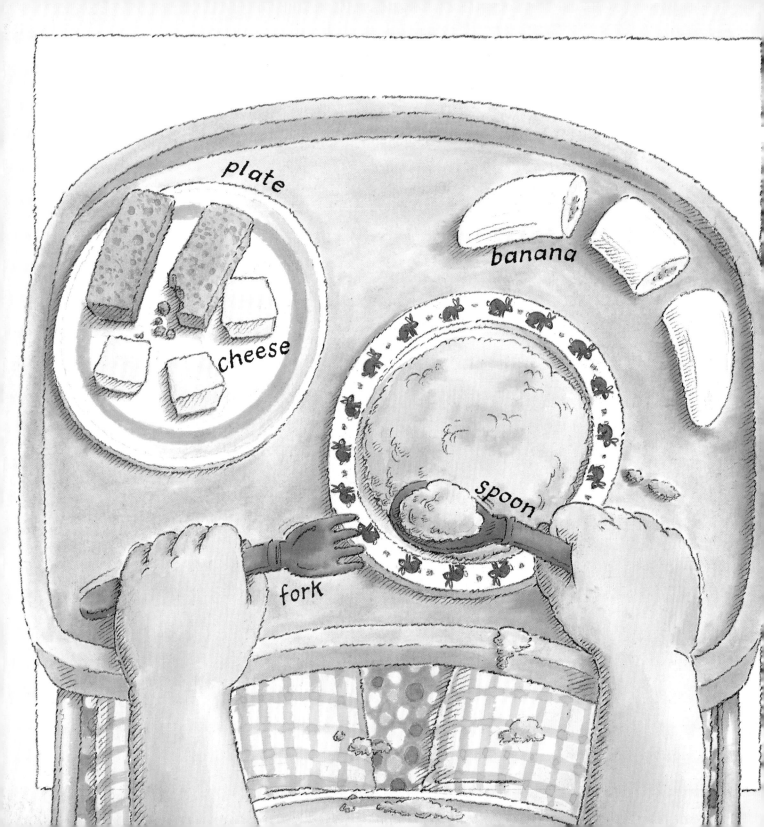

highchair

bib

bottle

bowl

cup

bird

swing

butterfly

stroller

leaves

duck

squirrel

flowers

grass

dog

basket

kitten

birds

fish

cat

rabbits

milk

shampoo

toothpaste

toothbrush

washcloth

brush

soap

sponge

towel

mobile

light

crib

teddy

slippers

book

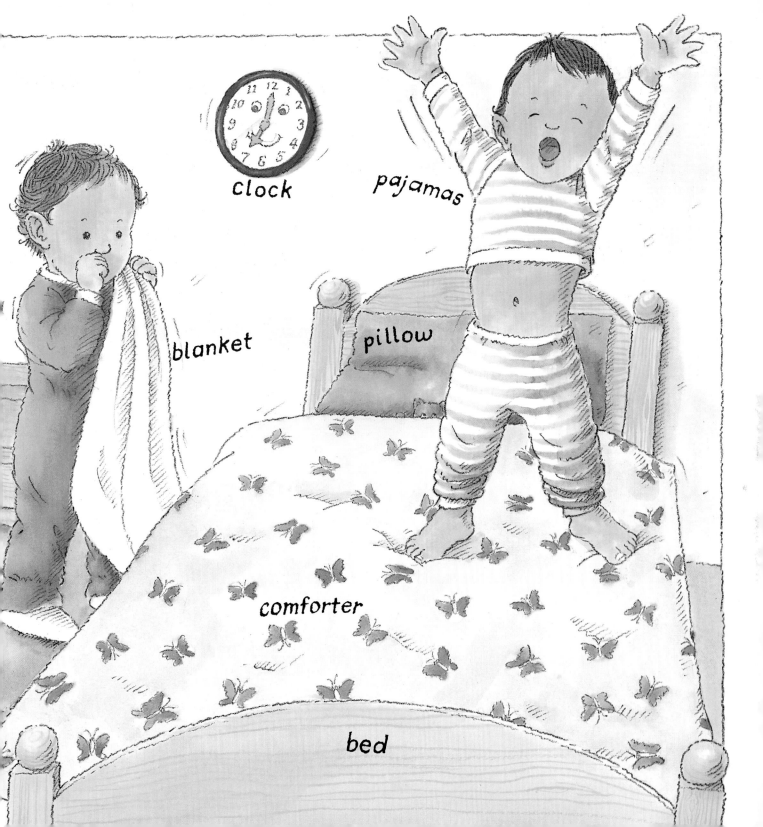

clock

pajamas

blanket

pillow

comforter

bed